OCT 12

PLAY BALL
BASEBALL

OUTFIELDERS

ICHIRO
51

By Jason Glaser

Must
Read!

Gareth Stevens
Publishing

Please visit our Web site, www.garethstevens.com. For a free color catalog of all our high-quality books, call toll free 1-800-542-2595 or fax 1-877-542-2596.

Library of Congress Cataloging-in-Publication Data

Glaser, Jason.
Outfielders / Jason Glaser.
   p. cm. — (Play ball. Baseball)
Includes index.
ISBN 978-1-4339-4492-5 (pbk.)
ISBN 978-1-4339-4493-2 (6-pack)
ISBN 978-1-4339-4491-8 (library binding)
1. Fielding (Baseball)—Juvenile literature. 2. Outfielders (Baseball)—Juvenile literature. I. Title.
GV870.G55 2011
796.357'25—dc22

2010030690

First Edition

Published in 2011 by
Gareth Stevens Publishing
111 East 14th Street, Suite 349
New York, NY 10003

Designer: Andrea Davison-Bartolotta
Editor: Greg Roza

Photo credits: Cover, p. 1 Otto Greule Jr./Getty Images; (cover, back cover, pp. 2, 3, 5, 7, 11, 12–13, 14–15, 17, 19, 21, 22–23, 25, 26–27, 33, 35, 37, 44–48 background image on all) pp. 9 (both), 42, 43 Shutterstock.com; p. 4 (both) Kidwiler Collection/Diamond Images/Getty Images; p. 5 NY Daily News Archive/Getty Images; pp. 6, 7 Buyenlarge/Getty Images; p. 8 Rogers Photo Archive/Getty Images; pp. 10, 11 Robert Riger/Getty Images; p. 12 Photo File/ MLB Photos/Getty Images; p. 13 C&G Collections/Getty Images; pp. 14, 35, 39 Stephen Dunn/Getty Images; p. 15 Jed Jacobsohn/Allsport/Getty Images; pp. 16, 33 Scott Boehm/ Getty Images; pp. 18, 32 Christian Petersen/Getty Images; p. 19 John Williamson/MLB Photos/Getty Images; p. 20 Bob Levey/Getty Images; p. 21 Mitchell Layton/Getty Images; p. 22 Michael DeHoog/Sports Imagery/Getty Images; p. 23 Jamie Squire/Getty Images; pp. 24, 30 J. Meric/Getty Images; p. 26 Photo File/Getty Images; p. 27 Jim McIsaac/Getty Images; p. 28 Jeff Gross/Getty Images; p. 29 Joe Robbins/Getty Images; p. 31 G. Newman Lowrance/ Getty Images; p. 34 Jeff Haynes/AFP/Getty Images; p. 36 Al Bello/Getty Images; p. 37 Jonathan Daniel/Getty Images; p. 38 Dilip Vishwanat/Getty Images; p. 40 Elsa/Getty Images; p. 41 Thinkstock.com; p. 44 Brian Bahr/Getty Images; p. 45 Thomas E. Witte/Getty Images.

Printed in the United States of America

CPSIA compliance information: Batch #CW11GS: For further information contact Gareth Stevens, New York, New York at 1-800-542-2595.

CONTENTS

The Deep Defenders 4

01: Following the
    Bouncing Ball 6

02: Choice Fielders 10

03: Out in the Outfield 16

04: The Best
    in the Business 34

05: Future Star: You! 40

Record Book 44

Glossary 46

For More Information 47

Index 48

Boldface words appear in the glossary.

4

The Deep Defenders

Good outfielders use smarts and strength to stop long hits from becoming runs or extra bases. A great outfielder can stop a runner from getting on base at all.

A Close Game

The 1954 World Series between the New York Giants and the Cleveland Indians had just begun. Game One was tied at 2 in the eighth **inning**, but the Indians had runners on first base and second base and no outs. The Cleveland batter, Vic Wertz, hit the ball so deep to center field that it seemed almost certain to bring in some runs.

Vic Wertz

Willie Mays

Giants center fielder Willie Mays bolted for the wall the moment Wertz hit the ball. He arrived just in time to catch the ball as it came down over his shoulder. He made a perfect throw back to second base, falling down as he did. It was a long, difficult throw that kept the runners from scoring. The Giants won the game 5–2. Many baseball fans believe it was "the Catch" made by Mays that allowed the Giants to win the series four games to none.

Outfielders have a lot of ground to cover to help their teams win. Read on to cover some ground yourself.

This series of photos shows Mays's famous catch and throw to second base.

① ② ③ ④ ⑤

Following the Bouncing Ball

As baseball rules changed over the years, the outfielder's job became more challenging. Of course, that also made it a lot more exciting!

Ball Control

In the earliest days of baseball, a game of "ball" could be started with a stick, a ball, and a handful of people. In these games, any number of players could take the field. Once the bases were covered, the rest ended up in the outfield. Games might have a dozen or more outfielders at once.

Union prisoners during the American Civil War play baseball.

An outfielder's job was to keep the ball from getting past him. Since outfielders didn't start wearing gloves until almost 1900, they usually fielded the ball on a hop or two instead of trying to catch it. Early baseball rules let outfielders make outs by catching the ball off one bounce. Even after the first professional team was formed in 1845 and the number of outfielders was set at three, balls could still be caught on the bounce for outs.

This picture from around 1900 shows an outfielder preparing to catch a ball "on the fly."

Pittsburgh
Pirates'
Paul Warner

At one time, baseball fields weren't surrounded by walls or boundaries. Batters had to hit to open spaces and run fast for a **home run**. With enclosed ball fields, batters could "hit one out of the park" for a home run. This was especially true once rules changed in the 1920s and 1930s to favor batting over pitching. Outfielders had to run faster after deep balls in hopes of keeping them in the ballpark. Any ball they caught was an out—even if they went over the wall themselves while catching it!

What Is the Live-Ball Era?

Prior to the 1920s, pitchers could scuff or moisten the surface of the baseball to make it fly in unpredictable ways. This made it difficult for batters to hit. Runs had to be scored by getting lucky hits or by advancing runners on steals. In 1920, the rules were changed to stop pitchers from altering the ball. This change made pitches easier to hit and batters started hammering home runs—which proved to be very popular with fans. This is how the "live-ball era" began.

8

To the Wall

In 1959, official distances were set for the outfield wall. It was to be at least 325 feet (99 m) from home plate on the sides and at least 400 feet (122 m) away in center field. Although many players were still able to hit the ball out of the park at those distances, it became much harder. Outfielders now had the opportunity to make more plays on deep balls.

400

outfield

325

325

Some outfielders wore extra large gloves in hopes of reaching higher and farther to catch more balls. In 1962, a rule was added that outlawed oversized gloves.

With a wide area to patrol, outfielders have a big challenge on defense. Here are some outfielders who have stepped up to that challenge.

Mr. Tiger

For more than 20 years, Detroit Tigers fans had no worries about balls hit to right field. The sure-handed Al Kaline made that spot his home for his whole career. Between 1953 and 1974, Kaline's skillful defense earned him 10 **Gold Glove** Awards and a World Series Championship. Kaline was and still is one of Detroit's most popular sports heroes.

Kaline prepares to make a catch during a game in 1964.

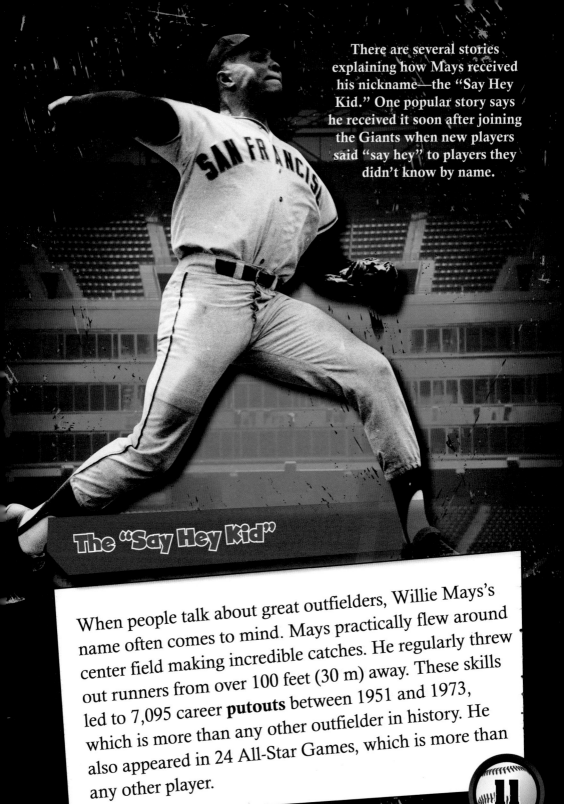

There are several stories explaining how Mays received his nickname—the "Say Hey Kid." One popular story says he received it soon after joining the Giants when new players said "say hey" to players they didn't know by name.

The "Say Hey Kid"

When people talk about great outfielders, Willie Mays's name often comes to mind. Mays practically flew around center field making incredible catches. He regularly threw out runners from over 100 feet (30 m) away. These skills led to 7,095 career **putouts** between 1951 and 1973, which is more than any other outfielder in history. He also appeared in 24 All-Star Games, which is more than any other player.

11

Willie Mays shared the record for Gold Glove Awards—12—with another fantastic outfielder, Roberto Clemente. Clemente started with the Pittsburgh Pirates in 1955 and won two championships there. He robbed many batters of hits and extra bases, regularly throwing out anyone who tried for a **double**. Clemente died in a plane crash in 1972 while delivering emergency supplies to Nicaragua following a terrible earthquake. In 1973, the **MLB** named their community service award after him.

Roberto Clemente

A Special Honor

Following Clemente's death, he was admitted into the National Baseball Hall of Fame. He is the only player to be named to the Hall of Fame without having been out of baseball for 5 years.

Mantle grew up in Commerce, Oklahoma. He was very good in sports and so fast that he earned the nickname the "Commerce Comet."

The Comet

Few ballplayers ran harder or faster to the ball than Mickey Mantle. The lifelong New York Yankee's quick hands were carried along on even faster feet. Many baseball fans remember Mantle for his batting. However, the center fielder also led the American League three times in **fielding percentage** in a career that lasted from 1951 to 1968. If a series of leg injuries hadn't slowed him down, Mantle might have been the greatest outfielder ever.

13

Charlie Hustle

What Pete Rose lacked in natural ability he made up for by playing hard. Rose hustled on every play for every ball, catching hits other outfielders would have let bounce. He played the ball well even at top speed. His lifetime fielding percentage of .991 is among the best ever.

Out of Left Field

In 1998, Barry Bonds won his eighth Gold Glove Award. No left fielder has won one since. Bonds's ability to sense the motion of the ball let him play batted balls off bounces and angles that few others could.

Faded Glory

The actions of Rose and Bonds off the field might keep them out of the Hall of Fame. Rose was accused of gambling on baseball games while playing and managing the Cincinnati Reds. Bonds has been accused of using illegal performance-enhancing drugs when he played. The fact that they were placed among the greatest baseball players ever before their troubles only makes their stories more disappointing.

In 1989, 19-year-old Ken Griffey Jr. was **Rookie** of the Year for the Seattle Mariners. He leaped across the outfield with grace to grab line drives, catch blooped fly balls, and yank high balls from the air. Twenty years later, after playing for other teams, he returned to Seattle to finish his career. He won 10 Gold Glove Awards and a league **MVP**.

Griffey Jr. throws ball to the infield ng a game against Cleveland Indians in 1995.

15

Out in the Outfield

Trying to keep baseballs from hitting the grass in an area as large as a ballpark outfield takes a combination of players with speed, strength, and skill. These players must work together as a unit on every play to make sure balls don't stay loose for long.

Ins and Outs

A baseball diamond is formed by a series of bases and the connecting base lines. Runners travel around the bases during the game and try to score. The area around these bases, marked by sand and dirt, is the infield. The outfield is the grassy area from the infield to the back wall and from the extended first base line to the extended third base line.

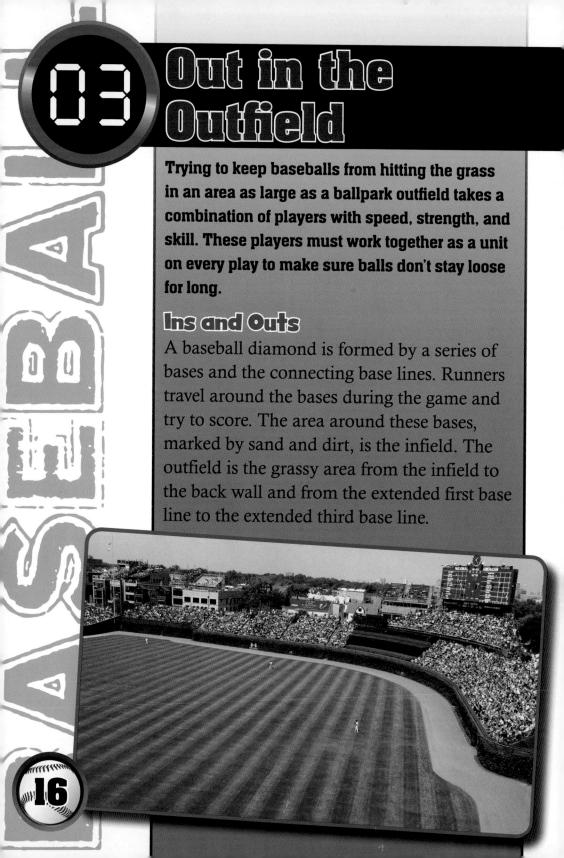

The Big Three

At most levels of baseball—including the pros—there are three outfielders. The outfield is divided into imaginary sections and named by their location in relation to home plate. The outfielder who covers the largest part of the field—the middle—is called the center fielder. The person covering the area on the third base side is the left fielder. The player covering the area on the first base side is the right fielder.

center field

left field

right field

second base

infield

third base

first base

home plate

DEFENSIVE FORMATIONS

When playing defense in baseball, being in the right position is the difference between outs and base hits, as well as the key to stopping runners from scoring. Outfielders always keep that in mind as they take the field on defense.

Basic Formation

Outfielders position themselves halfway between the infielders and the back wall. The left fielder covers the space between the third baseman and the shortstop. The center fielder covers the area between the shortstop and second baseman. The right fielder works the area between second base and first base. These positions cover the gaps between the infielders.

Tampa Bay Rays outfielders Carl Crawford, B. J. Upton, and Gabe Gross discuss strategy during a 2008 playoff game against the Boston Red Sox.

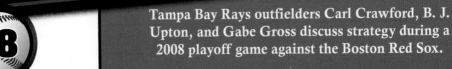

While playing against the Seattle Mariners, Texas Rangers center fielder Josh Hamilton backs up teammate Elvis Andrus.

Playing In

Sometimes one or more outfielders "plays in" by moving closer to the infield. Playing in can be helpful in close games where an outfielder needs to throw to home to stop a runner from scoring. It can also be used against weak hitters or on sides where a batter doesn't hit well. From an in position, outfielders can also back up infielders on **bunts** or infield hits. Playing in, however, can be dangerous because deep balls might go over the outfielders' heads.

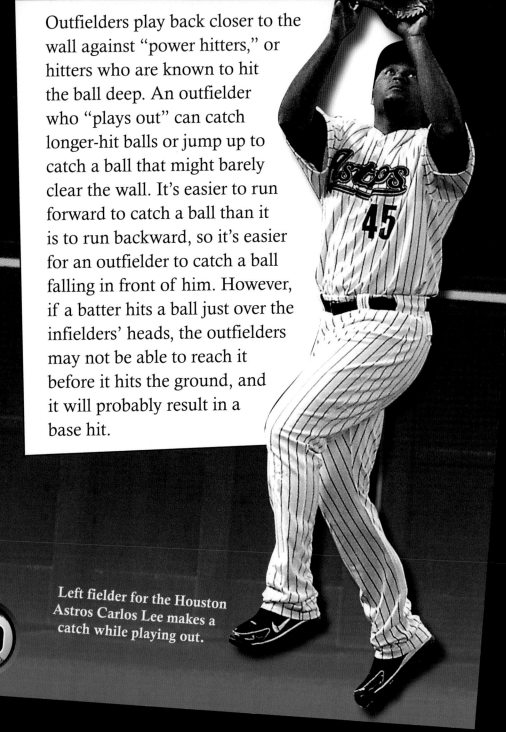

Outfielders play back closer to the wall against "power hitters," or hitters who are known to hit the ball deep. An outfielder who "plays out" can catch longer-hit balls or jump up to catch a ball that might barely clear the wall. It's easier to run forward to catch a ball than it is to run backward, so it's easier for an outfielder to catch a ball falling in front of him. However, if a batter hits a ball just over the infielders' heads, the outfielders may not be able to reach it before it hits the ground, and it will probably result in a base hit.

Left fielder for the Houston Astros Carlos Lee makes a catch while playing out.

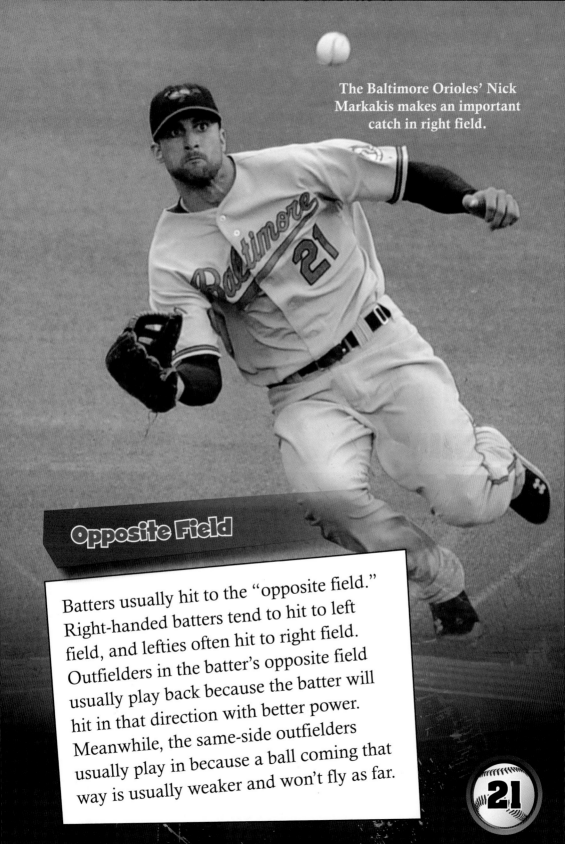

The Baltimore Orioles' Nick Markakis makes an important catch in right field.

Opposite Field

Batters usually hit to the "opposite field." Right-handed batters tend to hit to left field, and lefties often hit to right field. Outfielders in the batter's opposite field usually play back because the batter will hit in that direction with better power. Meanwhile, the same-side outfielders usually play in because a ball coming that way is usually weaker and won't fly as far.

21

Against batters who commonly hit to the opposite field, outfielders may use a **shift**. This means that all outfielders move sideways to better cover the area the batter is most likely to hit to. Against a right-hander, for example, the outfielders may shift closer to left field. This shrinks the area the outfielders need to cover and makes it more likely they can field the ball for an out.

Justin Upton, right fielder for the Arizona Diamondbacks, prepares to make a catch against the Florida Marlins.

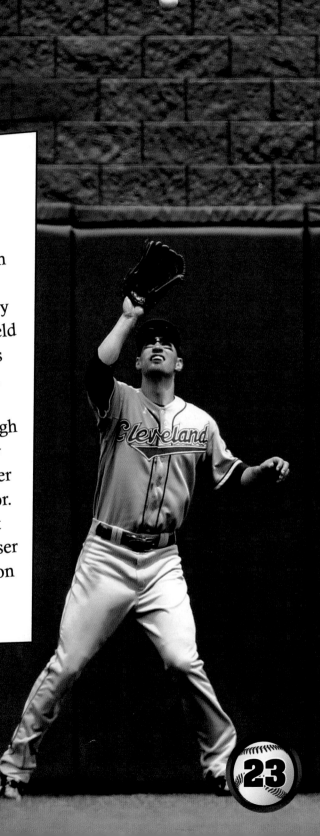

With runners on base, a batter doesn't want to hit to an area where the defense can easily throw the lead runner out. With a runner on second, for example, a batter may try to hit the ball to right field where the outfielder has to make a longer throw. If the outfielders know the batter is good enough to control his hits, they may shift to better cover the spot he's aiming for. Outfielders not in that area may creep in closer to back up infielders on the play.

The Cleveland Indians' center fielder Grady Sizemore is in the perfect position to catch a deep fly ball.

23

KEY SKILLS

Many of the skills needed to play outfield can be learned with hard work and practice. Here's what an outfielder needs to work on.

The Jump Start

A well-positioned outfielder needs to be moving when the ball is hit. To get going quickly, an outfielder starts with his feet pointed at home plate, shoulder width apart. From a crouch, the outfielder drops his hands slightly behind him, ready to move as the pitch is thrown. Based on the location of the pitch and the batter's swing, the outfielder can target where the ball is likely to go.

Ben Zobrist of the Tampa Bay Rays catches a ball while running toward the wall.

Once the ball is hit, it's all about speed. For a high fly ball, the outfielder moves underneath for a catch as it comes down. For a **line drive** or a low hit ball, outfielders must get in front of it and not let it pass. Good outfielders should move at full speed, either to catch the ball or field it. The quicker the ball gets into the outfielder's glove, the sooner he can throw it back to the infield.

foul line →

foul line
↓

Fair and Foul

Outfielders have to be able to cover the area outside the foul lines, too. If an outfielder catches a foul ball, the batter is out.

25

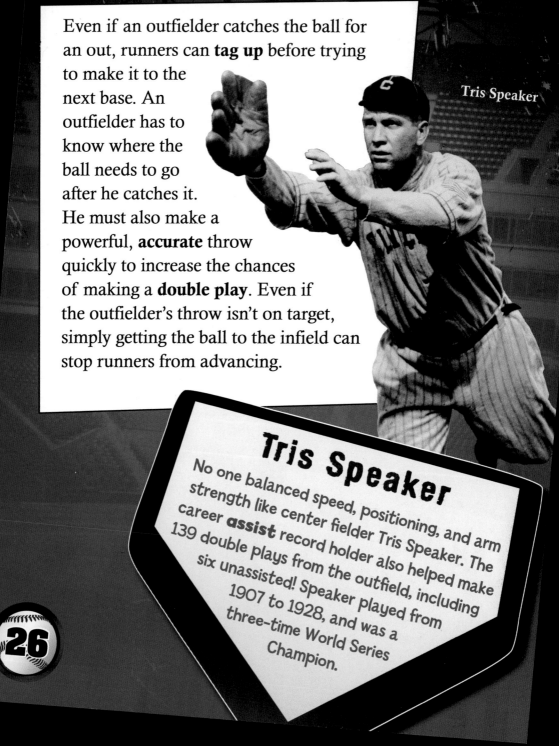

Even if an outfielder catches the ball for an out, runners can **tag up** before trying to make it to the next base. An outfielder has to know where the ball needs to go after he catches it. He must also make a powerful, **accurate** throw quickly to increase the chances of making a **double play**. Even if the outfielder's throw isn't on target, simply getting the ball to the infield can stop runners from advancing.

Tris Speaker

Tris Speaker

No one balanced speed, positioning, and arm strength like center fielder Tris Speaker. The career **assist** record holder also helped make 139 double plays from the outfield, including six unassisted! Speaker played from 1907 to 1928, and was a three-time World Series Champion.

Outfielders Carlos Beltrán (left) and Ryan Church of the New York Mets discuss a play as they leave the field during a game against the Pittsburgh Pirates.

Backup and Cutoff

Outfielders have a job on every hit. If they can't get to a ball, they may need to back up a fielder who can in case that fielder misses it. They may need to act as the **cutoff** thrower between a deep outfielder and a baseman. During throws within the infield, outfielders back up the basemen in case wild throws get past them.

27

COMMUNICATE

Outfielders need to communicate well during play. Shifts and cutoffs only work when everyone knows where to be.

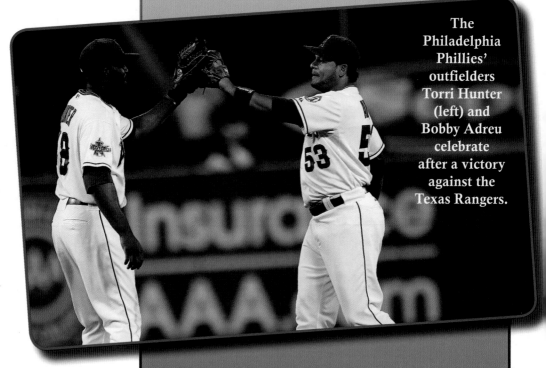

The Philadelphia Phillies' outfielders Torri Hunter (left) and Bobby Adreu celebrate after a victory against the Texas Rangers.

Pecking Order

In most cases, the center fielder sets the defensive position and the others follow him. Having the best view of home plate lets him see the batter's **stance**, what pitches the catcher calls for, and other defensive clues. Outfielders often use hand motions to tell each other how far to move and where to stand before the next pitch.

Center fielder Matt Kemp with the Los Angeles Dodgers calls for a catch to avoid running into his fellow outfielders.

The Warning Track

Another thing outfielders try to avoid is running into the wall while chasing a ball. Most ballparks have several feet of dirt instead of grass just before the fences. This "warning track" lets outfielders know the wall is near.

Watch Out!

When a fly ball is hit between two outfielders, both players might run to catch it. The center fielder is usually responsible for making the play. Still, any outfielder who goes for the ball should signal or yell out that he can make the catch. The other fielder then backs up the player who called the catch. This way, the caller can go for the ball without worrying about running into his teammate.

29

LOVE THE GLOVE

Above all else, an outfielder must catch the ball! The slightest drop or bobble will give the offense extra bases and runs.

Catch and Release

Young baseball players are taught to catch the ball with the glove hand and trap it in the glove with the bare hand. However, major league outfielders practice hours a day catching and picking up balls with their gloves. Instead of covering the ball in the glove with the throwing hand, outfielders clamp the ball tight with the glove hand and bring it up to the throwing hand, which is already up near the shoulder. This way the outfielder can catch and throw the ball faster.

The Tampa Bay Rays' Carl Crawford makes a throw after catching the ball during a game against the Florida Marlins.

Sometimes even the best positioning won't get an outfielder into place to make a catch without jumping. Even on a dead run, outfielders try to push off and up with both feet underneath the path the ball is traveling. To get the glove as high as possible, an outfielder stretches his glove hand up while tilting his other shoulder down toward his waist. Shifting the shoulders gives the extra bit of height to the outfielder's glove hand.

Jacoby Ellsbury of the Boston Red Sox makes a leaping catch in a game against the Kansas City Royals.

BEFORE THE GAME

Outfielders need to study almost as hard as managers! Preparing to play outfield is a mix of brain and muscle power.

New York Yankees outfielder Curtis Granderson knew exactly where to stand to catch this ball for an out.

Removing the Guesswork

Professional outfielders keep charts that show where the other team's batters have been hitting the ball. Studying these charts tells outfielders where that batter is likely to hit. Teams design a game plan on how to pitch to each batter to keep the batter from hitting and how to be ready to field the ball if he does.

Trying to track a baseball in flight can be difficult, especially when the sun, clouds, lights, and other distractions interfere with the outfielder's vision. As outfielders play and practice, they listen to the sounds bats make. A sharp crack or dull thump can tell an outfielder how far, how fast, and even what direction the ball will fly!

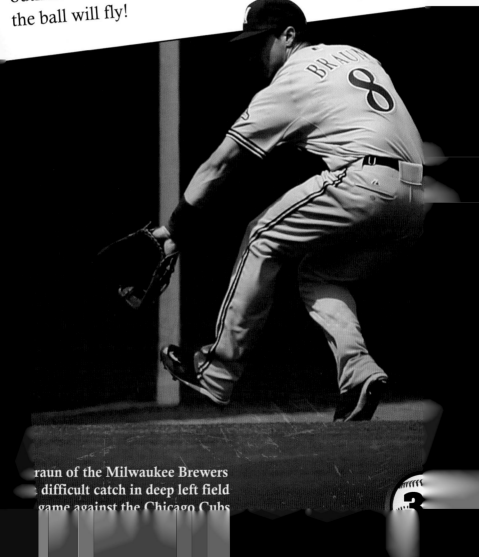

...raun of the Milwaukee Brewers
...difficult catch in deep left field
...game against the Chicago Cubs

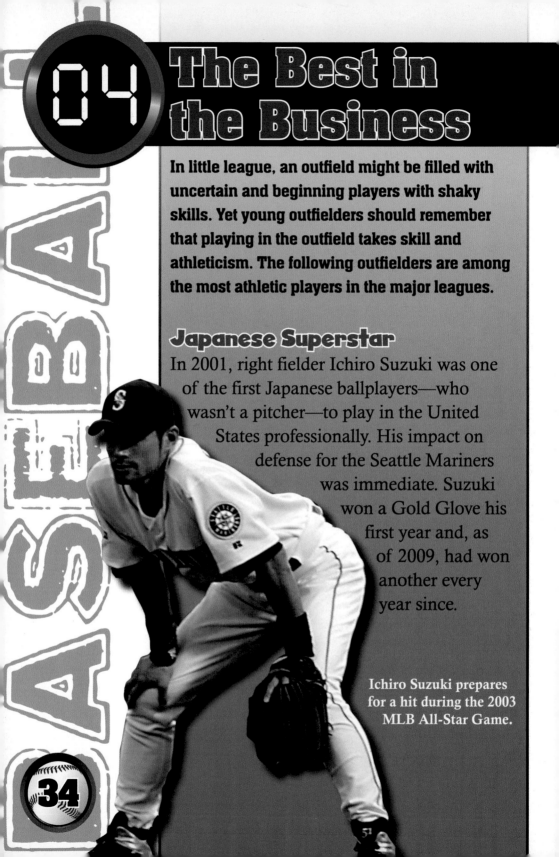

04

The Best in the Business

In little league, an outfield might be filled with uncertain and beginning players with shaky skills. Yet young outfielders should remember that playing in the outfield takes skill and athleticism. The following outfielders are among the most athletic players in the major leagues.

Japanese Superstar

In 2001, right fielder Ichiro Suzuki was one of the first Japanese ballplayers—who wasn't a pitcher—to play in the United States professionally. His impact on defense for the Seattle Mariners was immediate. Suzuki won a Gold Glove his first year and, as of 2009, had won another every year since.

Ichiro Suzuki prepares for a hit during the 2003 MLB All-Star Game.

Another amazing outfielder who has won a Gold Glove year after year beginning in 2001 is Torii Hunter. He first played center field with the Minnesota Twins and then with the Los Angeles Angels of Anaheim. Hunter captured flies so easily that another ballplayer once called him "Spider-Man." Whether he's going deep toward the wall or playing in, Hunter rarely misses a chance to catch a ball that's hit to center field.

Torii Hunter steals a home run from Mike Cameron of the Boston Red Sox.

Carlos Beltrán—who was Rookie of the Year in 1999—began his career with the Kansas City Royals. It wasn't until he started playing for the New York Mets in 2005 that he began having his best seasons. In 2006 and 2008, Beltrán turned in the best fielding-percentage seasons in his career. His powerful throwing arm helped him win three straight Gold Gloves. A knee injury kept Beltrán from playing for a fourth in 2010.

In 2008, Beltrán had 418 putouts—more than any other center fielder in the National League.

Andruw Jones used to move into position to catch a ball with such calm and ease that some coaches thought he wasn't trying hard enough. His results spoke for themselves. Since his first professional game in 1996 at age 19, Jones has won 10 Gold Glove Awards as an outfielder and has a .990 career fielding percentage.

During a game against the Baltimore Orioles, Andruw Jones makes a fly-ball catch look easy.

37

As of 2010, Shane Victorino had the highest fielding percentage of any center fielder in the league (.996).

The Flyin' Hawaiian

Shane Victorino of the Philadelphia Phillies has speed that must be seen to be believed. He can cross the field to catch line drives that other fielders have to play off a bounce. His effort and skill have earned him two Gold Gloves since 2003. He has also won enough fans to be the first Hawaiian-born outfielder to play in an All-Star Game.

Never Give Up

Jim Edmonds is a player willing to do whatever it takes to catch the ball. Since 1993, Edmonds has been crashing his body against the ground or the wall to catch fly balls and make outs. Refusing to let balls go by has brought Edmonds eight Gold Glove Awards, one World Series Championship, and many highlight plays in his full career.

Jim Edmonds makes a diving catch in a game against the Houston Astros.

39

Future Star: You!

Looking to defend the outfield? Here are some things to practice so that you can take down the long ball.

The Overhead Catch

To catch a fly ball, try to stand where the ball would meet you at chest level coming down. Hold your glove up and out from your chest, but not high enough that you can't see the ball over it. Turn your hand so the ball will hit the glove's webbing, rather than hitting your palm and falling out. Keep your strong leg slightly behind you for balance. Clamp your bare hand on top of your glove to keep the ball inside.

Even after making an overhead catch, an outfielder needs to be prepared to make a throw to an infielder.

The drop step may seem awkward at first, but it will get easier with practice.

The Drop Step

Beginning players sometimes chase balls hit overhead by running backwards. They often end up falling down. Instead, take a step in the direction the ball is traveling. If the ball is hit to your right, step with the right foot. If it's hit to your left, step with your left foot. Turn that foot out away from your body as you step. Next, step across your body with the opposite foot. This "drop step" will get you moving forward after the ball. It also allows you to keep your eyes on the ball for the entire play.

When you play the outfield, it's just as important to be able to grab balls after a bounce as it is to snag flies. Have a friend hit or throw low balls to you. Allow the ball to hit the ground even if you can catch it. Instead, position yourself where you can catch it on the first bounce. Try to catch the ball on the way up. This exercise will help you judge how high and far hit balls will bounce. Balls you can't catch before the bounce in a game will be easier for you to field.

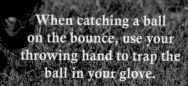

When catching a ball on the bounce, use your throwing hand to trap the ball in your glove.

An outfielder has to be ready for anything, whether it's a grounder or a fly ball.

Charge!

On a **grounder**, an outfielder can't wait for the ball if he wants to stop runners from advancing. Practice running up to grounders with the ball on your glove side. Make sure you have time to slow down and get in position as you get close. Turn your glove so the top brushes along the ground. The webbing will act like a ramp for the ball to climb into your glove.

USE YOUR BODY

Outfielders need to keep the ball in front of their body as they field. If the ball misses or goes off the glove, the outfielder's body can keep it from getting away.

Record Book

Baseball is a game that's played on the field but lives on in statistics. Let's take a look at some of the great achievements by outfielders.

Highest Career Fielding Percentage for an Outfielder:

1. Shane Victorino *(still active)*	OF	.9959	*(as of 9/30/10)*
2. Darin Erstad	CF/LF	.9955	
3. Brian Downing	LF	.9954	
4. Darryl Hamilton	OF	.9949	
5. Darren Lewis	CF	.9944	

Most Seasons with a Perfect Fielding Percentage for an Outfielder:

1. Brett Butler	CF	3
Darryl Hamilton	OF	3
Mickey Stanley	CF	3
Terry Puhl	RF/OF	3
5. *10 players*	OF	2

Most Seasons with Highest Fielding Percentage for an Outfielder:

1. Al Kaline	RF	7
2. George Foster	LF	6
Paul O'Neill	RF	6
4. Tim Raines Sr.	LF	5
Darren Lewis	CF	5
Amos Otis	CF	5
John "Pop" Corkhill	OF	5
Mike Griffin	OF	5

Darin Erstad

Ken Griffey Jr.

Career Assists by an Outfielder:

1. Tris Speaker	CF	449
2. Ty Cobb	CF	392
3. Jimmy Ryan	OF	375
4. George Van Haltren	CF	349
5. Tom Brown	OF	348

Most Gold Glove Awards by an Outfielder:

1. Roberto Clemente	RF	12
Willie Mays	CF	12
3. Ken Griffey Jr.	CF	10
Andruw Jones *(still active)*	CF	10
Al Kaline	RF	10

All-Star Appearances by an Outfielder:

1. Hank Aaron	RF	25
2. Willie Mays	CF	24
3. Carl Yastrzemski	LF	18
4. Ted Williams	LF	17
Pete Rose	OF	17

45

Glossary

accurate: on target

assist: having touched the ball on a play in which an out is made

bunt: when a batter uses his bat to softly tap the pitch into play instead of using a full swing

cutoff: placing oneself between a thrower and the end target in order to catch and throw the ball on for a faster delivery

defense: the team trying to stop the other team from scoring

double: when a batter safely reaches second base after a hit

double play: a situation where two outs result from a hit ball

fielding percentage: a measure of a fielder's ability, determined by adding putouts and assists, and dividing that number by putouts, assists, and errors

Gold Glove: an award given each year to the player with the highest fielding percentage at each defensive position in each league

grounder: a hit ball that rolls or bounces along the ground

home run: when a batter runs around all the bases and reaches home plate after a hit, scoring a run

inning: a unit of play where each baseball team gets a chance to bat until three outs have occurred. A professional baseball game has nine innings.

line drive: a hard-hit ball that travels in a nearly straight line

MVP: most valuable player

MLB: Major League Baseball, the professional league for baseball in the United States and Canada

offense: the team trying to score

putout: to get a batter or runner out

rookie: a player during his first year playing professionally

shift: to change fielding position

stance: the way a batter stands while waiting for a pitch

tag up: to touch a base so that the runner may legally advance to the next base

For More Information

Books

Dreier, David. *Baseball: How It Works.* Mankato, MN: Capstone Press, 2010.

Healy, Nick. *Roberto Clemente: Baseball Legend.* Mankato, MN: Capstone Press, 2006.

Jacobs, Greg. *The Everything Kids' Baseball Book.* Avon, MA: Adams Media, 2010.

Kelley, James. *Baseball.* New York, NY: DK Publishing, 2010.

Mercado, Nancy. *Baseball Crazy.* New York, NY: Puffin Books, 2009.

Scaletta, Kurtis. *Mudville.* New York, NY: Alfred A. Knopf, 2009.

Web Sites

Club MLB
web.clubmlb.com
Major League Baseball's activity-filled site has games and interactive fun features to teach kids about baseball and its past and present players.

Kids' Club
mlb.mlb.com/mlb/kids/index.jsp
Major League Baseball's information site for kids who want to learn more about how to be a better player or want to write to their favorite player. The site also provides links to the pages of each Major League Baseball team.

National Baseball Hall of Fame
baseballhall.org
The Web site for the National Baseball Hall of Fame in Cooperstown, New York, tells the in-depth history of the game. Learn about the achievements of some of the finest players and personalities from more than 200 hundred years of baseball.

Index

Aaron, Hank 45
All-Star Games 11, 34, 38, 45

Beltrán, Carlos 27, 36
Bonds, Barry 14
Brown, Tom 45
Butler, Brett 44

center field 4, 5, 9, 11, 13, 17, 18, 19, 23, 26, 28, 29, 35, 36, 38, 44, 45
Clemente, Roberto 12, 45
Cobb, Ty 45
Corkhill, John "Pop" 44

Downing, Brian 44

Edmonds, Jim 39
Erstad, Darin 44

fielding percentage 13, 14, 36, 37, 38, 44
Foster, George 44

Gold Glove Awards 10, 12, 14, 15, 34, 35, 36, 37, 38, 39, 45
Griffey, Ken, Jr. 15, 45
Griffin, Mike 44

Hamilton, Darryl 44
Hunter, Torii 28, 35

Jones, Andruw 37, 45

Kaline, Al 10, 44, 45

left field 14, 17, 18, 20, 21, 22, 33, 44, 45
Lewis, Darren 44

Mantle, Mickey 13
Mays, Willie 4, 5, 11, 12, 45

O'Neill, Paul 44
Otis, Amos 44

Puhl, Terry 44

Raines, Tim, Sr. 44
right field 10, 17, 18, 21, 22, 23, 34, 44, 45
Rose, Pete 14, 45
Ryan, Jimmy 45

Speaker, Tris 26, 45
Stanley, Mickey 44
Suzuki, Ichiro 34

Van Haltren, George 45
Victorino, Shane 38, 44

Williams, Ted 45

Yastrzemski, Carl 45

About the Author

Jason Glaser is a freelance writer and stay-at-home father living in Mankato, Minnesota. He has written over fifty nonfiction books for children, including books on sports stars such as Jackie Robinson. As a youngster playing youth baseball, he once completed an unassisted triple play, which is the highlight of his sports career.